PRODUCTS: FROM IDEA TO MARKET

Snack Chips

FOCUS READERS®
BEACON

by Abby Doty

www.focusreaders.com

Copyright © 2025 by Focus Readers®, Mendota Heights, MN 55120. All rights reserved. No part of this book may be reproduced or utilized in any form or by any means without written permission from the publisher.

Focus Readers is distributed by North Star Editions:
sales@northstareditions.com | 888-417-0195

Produced for Focus Readers by Red Line Editorial.

Photographs ©: Shutterstock Images, cover, 1, 6, 8, 11, 12, 16, 19, 20, 22, 25; iStockphoto, 4, 26; Matt Sayles/Invision for Frito-Lay/AP Images, 15, 29

Library of Congress Cataloging-in-Publication Data
Library of Congress Cataloging-in-Publication Data is available on the Library of Congress website.

ISBN
979-8-88998-405-4 (hardcover)
979-8-88998-433-7 (paperback)
979-8-88998-486-3 (ebook pdf)
979-8-88998-461-0 (hosted ebook)

Printed in the United States of America
Mankato, MN
012025

About the Author

Abby Doty is a writer, editor, and booklover from Minnesota.

Table of Contents

CHAPTER 1
Fantastic Flavors 5

CHAPTER 2
Finding New Ideas 9

THAT'S AMAZING!
Customers' Choice 14

CHAPTER 3
Chip Factories 17

CHAPTER 4
Company to Customer 23

Focus Questions • 28
Glossary • 30
To Learn More • 31
Index • 32

CHAPTER 1

Fantastic Flavors

A girl and her brother want some snacks. Their dad comes in the door. He bought two bags of potato chips at the grocery store. The bright bags show different flavors.

Some chips come in small bags. Others come in big bags for sharing.

▷ **Some chips are thick and have ridges.**

One bag is full of barbecue chips. The other has dill pickle chips. Both flavors are new to the kids. They've never tried those chips before.

The girl tastes the barbecue chips. The chips are sweet and salty. They taste just like barbecue sauce. Her brother tries the dill chips. They really taste like pickles. Both kinds are delicious. The kids eat more. The girl wonders how the chips can taste so amazing.

Did You Know?
Potato chips were invented in the 1800s. They became widely popular in the 1920s.

CHAPTER 2
Finding New Ideas

New chip flavors come out every year. Snack companies often study food **trends**. They notice which flavors are popular. For example, pumpkin spice is trendy in fall.

Some chip companies make hundreds of flavors.

A company may make pumpkin spice chips at that time.

Different chip companies compete for the same **customers**. So, companies may copy similar businesses. They often release the same regular flavors. For example, most chip companies offer sour cream and onion chips.

But companies also try to stand out. They may choose unusual flavors. Flavor houses can help. These groups create new tastes.

A truffle flavor of a major chip brand is popular in Thailand.

Then food businesses can use those flavors. Companies also choose new ideas based on different sets of customers. Many companies create chips for **target audiences**.

Companies may want to hear from a large number of testers.

For example, some buyers focus on health. Companies can create healthier chips for these buyers. Companies may also create flavors to sell in different places.

After choosing an idea, workers make small batches. The chips go to food testers. These people give their feedback. They state their opinions about the chips' taste and feel.

Food scientists can adjust their recipe. They may add more of some **ingredients**. They may remove others. The process continues until the new chip is perfect.

Did You Know?
A chip recipe may need months of testing.

THAT'S AMAZING!

Customers' Choice

In 2012, the company PepsiCo launched "Do Us a Flavor." The project chose new flavors for Lay's chips. The company asked people to suggest new flavors. Customers sent in nearly four million ideas.

Judges chose three ideas. They were cheesy garlic bread, sriracha, and chicken and waffles. Lay's made those chips. They sold the chips in stores. Customers tasted them. Then, customers voted for their favorite. Cheesy garlic bread won. The woman who came up with the idea won $1 million.

The winner of the Lay's contest (left) attends a special event after the voting ended.

CHAPTER 3

Chip Factories

After perfecting a recipe, companies produce their chips. They gather ingredients. Many chips are made from potatoes. Companies bring potatoes from farms to factories.

Machines in a factory carry potatoes from one area to another.

After that, machines wash and peel the potatoes. Blades cut potatoes into thin slices. Then machines fry the slices in hot oil.

Adding flavor comes next. Food scientists create the seasonings. Sometimes, spice mixes come from real food. Other times, they include **artificial** flavors. Machines help add these flavors. They cover the chips. Finally, machines divide the chips into small groups. They pack chips into bags.

Machines divide and weigh potato chips.

Tortilla chips are another type of chip. This kind is made from corn. First, machines clean the corn. Then it soaks in water and chemicals. That helps remove the corn's husks.

Large factories can make thousands of chips every hour.

It softens the corn, too. Next, machines grind up the corn. That makes a dough. The dough is called masa.

Sharp tools cut the masa into shapes. These pieces are baked and fried. Finally, the machines season and package the chips.

When the bags of chips are ready, companies send them out. Workers pack the bags into large boxes. Trucks move the boxes. They go to **retailers**. Customers can buy the chips in stores.

Did You Know?
Some companies make chips from other vegetables. They may use sweet potatoes, carrots, or kale.

CHAPTER 4
Company to Customer

Companies need customers to buy their chips. So, they **advertise** to buyers. Businesses may advertise through packaging. For example, a chip might use healthy ingredients. Its bag could point that out.

 Companies want their packaging to stand out from other chips.

Customers who prefer natural chips can see that. Then they may buy the chips.

In some stores, cheaper chips go on lower shelves. Kids see those chips more easily. So, companies may use bright and colorful packages for cheap chips. These features catch the kids' eyes. Chips with fancier packaging might be higher up. These chips cost more money. But adults may like the fancier designs.

Some chips come in tubes instead of bags.

Chip packaging can stand out in other ways. For example, some bags have clear windows. Customers can see the chips inside. Other times, chip **brands** use dark colors. Most chip bags are bright.

25

Many chip buyers like to try lots of different flavors.

That means dark bags may stand out on the shelves.

Chip companies also reach customers with **commercials**. These ads show how tasty the chips are. They may show celebrities eating the product. Customers who like the celebrities may be more likely to buy the chips. Releasing many new products can help, too. Some companies put out several flavors each year. They hope to have a chip for everyone.

Did You Know?
Some companies make bags using less plastic. The change is good for the planet. It saves millions of pounds of plastic.

Focus Questions

Write your answers on a separate piece of paper.

1. Write a few sentences explaining the main ideas of Chapter 4.
2. If you could make a new chip flavor, what would it taste like?
3. What is one way that companies come up with new chip flavors?
   - **A.** by making chips in a factory
   - **B.** by looking at food trends
   - **C.** by making a chip commercial
4. Why would testing be important when creating new foods?
   - **A.** Testing can help improve the foods.
   - **B.** Testing can help advertise the foods.
   - **C.** Testing can help keep the foods the same.

5. What does **compete** mean in this book?

*Different chip companies **compete** for the same customers. So, companies may copy similar businesses.*

    A. hire workers in factories
    B. start new chip companies
    C. try to gain or win something

6. What does **feedback** mean in this book?

*These people give their **feedback**. They state their opinions about the chips' taste and feel.*

    A. thoughts
    B. money
    C. company

Answer key on page 32.

Glossary

advertise
To make messages or videos about a product so customers want to buy it.

artificial
Made by humans instead of happening naturally.

brands
Companies that are known for making products or services.

commercials
Messages or videos to sell a product. They appear during other programs.

customers
People who buy products.

ingredients
Foods that are mixed together to make a different food.

retailers
Businesses that sell products to customers.

target audiences
Groups of customers that a company wants to sell to.

trends
Things that are popular for a period of time.

To Learn More

BOOKS

Hill, Christina. *Supply Chains in Infographics*. Ann Arbor, MI: Cherry Lake Press, 2023.

Idzikowski, Lisa. *Robots in the Factory*. Minneapolis: Lerner Publications, 2024.

Wood, Alix. *How to Grow Potato Chips*. Minneapolis: Ruby Tuesday Books, 2024.

NOTE TO EDUCATORS

Visit **www.focusreaders.com** to find lesson plans, activities, links, and other resources related to this title.

Index

A
advertising, 23, 26

B
brands, 25

C
commercials, 26
customers, 10–11, 14, 21, 23–27

F
factories, 17–21
flavor houses, 10
flavors, 5–6, 9–12, 14, 18, 27
food scientists, 13, 18
food testers, 13

H
health, 12, 23–24

I
ingredients, 13, 17, 23

M
machines, 18–21
masa, 20

P
packaging, 23–25
potato chips, 5, 7, 17–18
potatoes, 17–18

R
retailers, 21

T
tortilla chips, 19–21
trends, 9

Answer Key: 1. Answers will vary; 2. Answers will vary; 3. B; 4. A; 5. C; 6. A